Love Me Louder:
A Family Portrait

Love Me Louder

Tyler Hurula

QUERENCIA

Querencia Press, LLC
Chicago Illinois

QUERENCIA PRESS

© Copyright 2022
Tyler Hurula

LIBRARY OF CONGRESS CATALOG-IN-PUBLICATION DATA

ISBN 979 8 9860788 3 0

www.querenciapress.com

First Published in 2022

**Querencia Press, LLC
Chicago IL**

Printed & Bound in the United States of America

CONTENTS

Bruises

I carry my mother's grief,
pickpocketed it as a child.

It kept growing and growing
and now it growls

from beneath my bones.
It began before I could bite—

when I could kick
her bruises from the inside out.

Secrets

If houses hold families,
and families have secrets,
my house was buzzing,

There is always chocolate
in the back right corner
of Mom's side table next to her bed.

I keep the shower door cracked
open so I can catch anyone creeping
up, in case they want to stab me in the shower.

I pull my sister's hair
when I'm angry and then hug
her when she threatens to tell.

We hide in the closet listening to the sound
of skipped heartbeats, as Dad's erupting voice
ricochets, after every visit from our grandparents.

bubbling, and barely able to keep
the blue siding from bursting
with the bruise of our tight lips.

Dad hates it
when our grandparents
come to visit.

The boxed wine
in the garage is only for cooking,
so sometimes Dad goes on a liquid diet.

Mom only cooks homemade meals
when the Mormon
missionaries come over for dinner.

Biting Back

I used to count the silence between
each of your steps—my room
in the basement, I had the entire
house mapped by the way the floors

creaked under the weight of your feet.
I walked as if the concrete
itself was slowing
me down

to ensure
I stepped on every crack
in the sidewalk. Not to break
your back, but to even

everything out. I made sure to step
on just as many cracks
with my left foot
as I did with my right. I hoped

if I could keep everything balanced
I could keep your temper tethered.
During a tea party mishap,
my sister pressed my finger

to a piece of glass, and I bled crimson
drops on the stairway to find
you. Your hand printed purple stars
on her backside. The social worker

pulled me out of recess to ask
if it was true. I fucking lied

for you, Dad. I didn't know what else
to do. You drove me to high school

so early the sky was still bruised
black. I'd watch lights flash
by from your beat-up car,
speeding to match the violence

racing from your lips, daggers steered
in my direction. A single
silent tear slid down my face
and you said *that's right,*

cry, smart ass, cry.
And you know what? I do.
I cry all the time. I even have a shirt
that says crying is good for you

and I wear it like a big *fuck you*.
I have grown into my bad behavior.
I stole the *bitch* from your bite
and bent it backward until it broke.

God as Accomplice

The bishop of the Mormon Church
told my parents they had to get married
because they were living together,

and you can't live together unless
you're married because then you might
be tempted to see each other naked.

My *God* how terrible would that be?
More terrible than the day my dad's
fury chased our family to church.

He bolted through the chapel door
like a drunken Messiah, blue jeans
faded, kneeling next to us. Rage

radiated through him; there were heat
lines waving above him for the congregation
to see. Instead of shining light on his anger,

they enveloped us in another layer of sacred
secrecy, sliding us their backhanded bible full of
advice on how to stuff down our fear.

Better to keep him proselytizing his short
temper on our family-home-evenings than to
break this sacred covenant.

So Mad He Can't See Straight

Daddy tramples into the kitchen—
eyes bright, ablaze with accusations aiming
outward. I'm caught in the crosshairs.

There are two ways out
but we've already locked
eyes. He's loaded, though
I have yet to see the inside of a bottle.

He looks at me as my eyes leak
and tells me I have cat-shit
green eyes, and if I don't stop, he'll give

me something to cry about.
He's so mad he can't see straight,
and then he doesn't. His eyes go cross,
like the time I rolled mine and he

said they'd stick like that—but his
stick like that.
When my baby sister is born, he hates her

crying because she seems
to do it most when he is in the room.
He holds her tight, like one of those
keychains you squeeze and the eyes

pop out. My mom begs him
to let her go. As his anger grows,
so do his arms. They grow

and grow like they're being

squeezed and my sister slips
out and his arms are too big to hold
her. Dad crouches

with his still crossed
eyes in front of me and my sister.
The closet door came off

its hinges and he wants to know
who did it. My hands are the jello
in the fridge. Tremble seeps
through me as I eye the wooden

spoon splayed out in the pound
of his hands. His jaw juts,
incisors bared like a challenge.

His bottom teeth lengthen
into a lilac lattice fence,
and I paint pink pansies on it.
Fragile wings confetti

the hallway after he slingshot
the tv remote at my mom's
glass angel collection.

She tells me later she read
abusers don't actually lose
control. You can tell because
nothing he ever breaks is his

own. That night when his eyes bleed
clear apologies, I trace the lines
of his hands and watch the

hairs on his knuckles grow
thick and soft as they fleece
into teddy bear paws.
I tell him I have a girlfriend

when he asks if I've found
a boy at college yet. I see red rage
splotch in as he looks past

me in two different directions.
I guess I broke the closet
door on my way out after all,
and he hasn't forgotten. He raises

his oversized arms above his head
and his whole body inflates
with heat until he glitters

into a cloud of dust. The only thing left
is my footprints leading out the door.

Kickball Red

His face is beat red.
No. His face is red, but beat
here is a verb.

Not so much with his fists,
though he does that, too—just not to me.
He beats me with his words.

They slide hot and spiny—etch
into the soft of my throat and well
into my eyes. Pools too heavy,

so they slide down the porcelain
of my cheeks.
Break me into pieces.

His face is kickball red. Like the ones
at recess that sting when boys throw
them so hard they welt my chest.

The teacher says those boys like me.
My dad assures me he loves me.

His jaw is set—like a dog with an underbite,
straining against the chain holding
him back, but there is nothing

holding him back except
the butt of his chin.
We have the same chin.

His eyes are vacant—boring

into me with a not-quite-there
stare. His eyes are the color of dirt

after it rains, when worms wiggle,
waving like mad to get back
home. His eyes say no

one is home. I search them, reaching
my fingers forward toward his face and plead
for him to love me the way he promised to.

Hide-and-Seek

Hide and seek is stifled
        giggles–trying to keep quiet, covering
                mouths to muffle

the sticky-sweet thrill of being sought after. It's the secret to
entertaining
                    bored children when
                their parents are two hours late
    from their date, and you just want to go
home.

It's exploration that needs
                no explanation. To this day I can't stand
        hide-and-seek.
    It is the booming voicebox of my dad's cageless rage.
Rattled, I used to seek
        refuge in the closet, waiting for the
                                bang

        of his fist to rip a hole into the wall
                        exposing me.

    Every time I try the echoes of his fire eyes
        ripple
            in the tremor
                of my chest.

            His footsteps stomp icy in the shallow
        of my breath and I dare myself
to sit still--aching to leap out before

                        I am found.

Shattered

He was human once. I loved him
with the bruised-blind adoration

and ignorance of a self-proclaimed
Daddy's girl. He was still magic

then—made out of eucalyptus, incense,
the soaked-up knowledge of *every* book,

and probably unicorn horns. Like when he let
me ride on his back until I fell over in stitches.

My face still hurts from my smile. I laid
on his back every night staring up

while his whiskey-smooth voice plastered
stories onto the ceiling. I think he might

have been more heartbroken than me
when he couldn't afford my horse

riding lessons anymore. When Mom
was gone Saturdays, we cleaned together

and piled up on his bed in a tight
tangle of giggles, braids, and loose limbs.

I don't want to write this, but you have to know
how he cut a hole in my throat with the dullest

knife each time his fist punched through the wall
of my high expectations. I was filled to spilling

over with forgiveness each time he asked
for it. I was all pigtails and scraped

elbows. I couldn't deny this man on his knees,
holding my hand with guilt dripping down his face.

Basement

My bathroom is long—like a hallway.
The linoleum floor is lined with dead spiders,
legs up and tongues spilling out.

I imagine that last part because it makes it easier
to convince myself to scoop them up and flush them farewell.
The weekend my parents left town is when my shower

became a trap. The jaws of the glass doors kept me
confined, and I had to slide them two inches open so I could
keep watch because I was convinced Norman Bates

was going to come stab me. It was also the last weekend
my parents let me watch scary movies at my neighbor's
house.
My bathroom is connected to the bedroom and closet,

and it is all in the basement and I am all by myself.
I sleep in the top bunk even though my sister
moved out last year. I wake up and smash my skull

on the popcorn ceiling every morning.
I only go into my closet during the day. There is not enough
light to see in there and I am scared of the spiders

that scatter every time I open the door.
I hear everything down here. I hear the alarm
going off in my parents' room two floors above

me in the mornings, and I hear the sink in the kitchen
as the water snakes down the pipes. I hear
my dad burst in through the front door and for a moment

my stomach swings into the swamp of my seasick heart.
I can tell before the door slams shut that it wasn't
a good day and soon I know someone will have to pay.

Why I Hate Holidays: A Glimpse into Christmases Past

We are racing on the highway turned
speedway. I am in the back seat. Eyes as big
as pumpkin pie. Mom is white as The Ghost
of Christmas Past, and I am counting
each car we pass. Dad is driving
and says he's so mad he can't see straight
and I have to take him literally. The silence
bubbles from inside my chest around the words
none of us will say out loud.

The room is dim, and my sister and I are staring
at the straight faces and solemn eyes
of our parents. They announce Santa isn't real.
It's just mommy and daddy
and we are swimming in a snowstorm
of debt and Christmas is going to be small
this year. *Don't tell your other sisters*. Guilt feasts
on each bauble and trash bag filled full
of wrapping paper from the gifts
I know they found buried in their empty wallets.

My sister and I sneak upstairs each year
to glimpse each gift before the sun wakes
up. This year, we are fostering greyhounds
and forgot to let them in on our secret.
They don't see us, and growl
from their kennels and we are spooked
and go back to bed before they turn us in.

Grandma opens her gift on the couch. It could
have been a plate set or a box of brandy
stuffed chocolates or a rose-tinted tablecloth,

but I don't remember. I was excited
and belted out what a great deal it was
because I remember my mom being excited
about what a great deal it was. Both
of them back-hand me with their eyes,
build a box in my chest for me to bury
the shame wrapped into every dollar bill I'd ever see.

Grandma's dog leaps on the counter
and eats a huge chunk of the just dressed
turkey. Now she is yelling because she hates
cooking and today is ruined. She's wrong.
The ruin sneaks in soft at first. It begins
just after a blissful belly of candy at Halloween.
Dad's fist pockets the plywood walls
by the time we see Grandma. He hates her
more each year and I know because my house
has flooded with puddles of his outrage. At least
the dog got a treat.

Forgiveness has Eight Wobbly Legs

The couch had bruised
brushstroke stripes—purple
and a violent shade of rust,

crisscrossed as if punching
each other. Dad reached his roaring

hands around it and flipped
it upside down. It wobbled like a dead
bug twitching. Like the spider

I was too scared to smoosh
so I sprayed it with Windex over

and over until it crinkled
itself into a tiny tremble.
I really didn't want to hurt

something so much smaller than me.
Maybe that's why the couch landed

on the other side of the room.
Earlier that week a baby bird had fallen
from the rafters at my horse riding

lesson. Dad took off his own
shirt, and with a gentle

hand scooped this bald bird
up, and I carried it home on my lap.
The car crawled home to avoid any bumps

for this hollow-boned creature.
His strong and precise hands built

a makeshift nest and we did our best
to nurture it back to health. Both
our eyes spilled over as he laid

the bird in a shoebox coffin,
tucked it in under his shirt.

So, when I look back and ask myself
how I forgave him over and over
and over I remember his hands—

how they threw couches, yes,
and cradled dying birds, too.

Inheritance Disguised as Decision

My parents gave me a God on a brass
platter. The unhealthy dose of dread
came after—maybe that's why

they called us Latter Day Saints.
You get to wait until you're eight
years old before you're baptized

because then it's *your* decision. But what
eight-year-old is going to stand there and say
hey, I'd really like to know a little more

about this God guy and why He created man
in his image, but women are resolute
in their kneeling, crushed under the weight

of his rib? At eight years old I was flailing
around in the yard neighing and fighting
with my neighbor about who got to be the baby

horse and who had to be the mother.
Even then I was shirking off my maternal
duties to the church, not knowing

that was supposed to be my destiny.
They wrapped up my agency and labeled
it *faith,* engraved my name in gold on a garden

colored scripture case. Now my nephew
tells me I give off horse girl vibes,
must have felt how I fought my fealty

to a God I was coerced into believing in—
bucked it off my back with the force of a full
blown exorcism. At eight years old,

the only temple I'd known was outside
praying on a soft bed of green blades.
So, while I don't really know what my nephew

meant, I do know I would have done anything
for my parents when I was young enough
to come home with grass-stained knees.

My Mother's Leftovers

The only thing keeping me and my
sisters from eating my mom's leftovers
is her offensive habit of covering

everything with mushrooms.
No one can stomach the fuckery
of fungal flecked *food.*

Sometimes she threatens to cover
desserts with them to keep
unwanted fingers from feeling

their way through the Styrofoam free-
for-all in the fridge. I wouldn't
put it past her, either.

There are four young mouths
to feed and there is never
enough. I sneak upstairs

with soft feet and steal a sliver
of her scraps. I savor
each sweet stolen bite before

the guilt in my gut licks
my conscience clean, and I shove
the leftovers box into the back

of the fridge. As if burying it would
keep her from noticing I took
too much. Sometimes I gather

loose change from the couch and walk
to the store for a sandwich. I slice
it into squares and cling wrap each

one so I know I have something saved.
I stock up on chocolate milk from the free
lunch program. I drop my last

penny into the pond on my walk
to school wishing I had a love note
written on a post-it

from my mom like my friends,
but we can't afford
a lunch box to put it in.

Heirloom

The gut punch wasn't so much fist
as it was jawbreaker. Sweet and bright red
on the outside and so much more layered

than I could have understood as I watched
my mother in the bathroom. She was scaling
on her mascara, eyes the size of dinner plates

as she swiped the liquid onto her eyelashes, staring
into the mirror. I saw my reflection, head
miniscule over her shoulder. My bangs

were still growing back after my self-inflicted
haircut. I wore mismatched socks and an ugly
brown skirt she picked out for me. Her eyes flickered

in my direction only for a moment before
the words snaked out like honey—thick
and sticky. *Maybe you should suck in your stomach.*

She hid chocolate in her bedside table, and I would sneak
in when she wasn't home, listening
for the door lock twisting. I didn't want to get caught

stealing. I would only take two at a time and weigh
out each piece. I'd place them in my palm,
line them up on my stomach to see how much bigger

each one would make me grow.
I knew each bite was a promise
I couldn't keep. With delicate fingers, I'd unwrap

the dark blue foil and toss aside the note about life
or love as I didn't know much about either. I'd eat one
then, letting the chocolate melt on my tongue;

play a game with myself to see how long I could make
it last. I kept my own secret stash under my pillow.
I learned to hide food like I learned to hide my body.

I'd drown myself in the eggplant garment that looked
more like a bedsheet. Dad bought it for me from the plus-size
clothing store after the clerk told him I wasn't big enough

to fit in their clothes. I equated skinny with worthy
of their love and have only now learned I was only a mirror
reflecting their own fears–that I've never not been worthy of
love.

Self-Preservation

Pink heart shaped sticky notes
splatter the table as I gather
and shove them together to make

you a mouse. The humps of the heart
turn into the curves of his ears. I slap
two hearts together, pointy parts

out to make an oval for his body,
give him a toothpick knife
and draw bloodthirsty eyes.

I name him Norman Bates.
My eyes stick to his beady,
drawn-on eyes when you tell me a toothpick

knife wasn't the only weapon
you were fighting. Dad's temper ruptured
and this time it wasn't just his glass

shard words cutting you, but his actual
hand as he shoved you against the wall.
All for trying to pry him away from

our youngest sister, but his open
hand whipped out at anything too close.
        (You were too close.)

The night his violence left his lips
and leaped to his clenched fist
I was out with Mom. The blistering

ring of her phone cut
into our conversation. His screams
echoed through the speaker.

The rain banged bullets
against the car and his voice
was a loaded gun. Only I didn't realize

then it wasn't aimed at me—
and never would be. As the eldest,
I should have been your first line

of defense. Yet his roar seemed to slip
past me straight onto you. Under
the crushing bruise of guilt,

I sped from the scene of his crimes,
leaving you in his clenched fist.
        (I have never looked back.)

My Mother, the Artist

The first time he painted you black and blue I was still inside
        of you, kicking back against the radiant blows
of his fists. Shame stained your face as the nurse

 looked away when you told her you didn't fall
        down the stairs–her disdain blaming
you. So you kept this sick secret artfully stored in the strokes

of your solitude. You found healing in your art, canvassing
        away the commotion of him. Acrylics littered
the basement of our home. You became so good at blending

the pigments to hide the bruises. You created a façade–
        a family gallery for the world to see. A curated
collection of stippled-on smiles. I watched him throw his jet

black temper into the case with your glass dolls
        just before you dressed me up for church
in my stark dress. Your red raspberry-puree

of brush-stroked hair, a tangle of untamable
        curls, reaching out to grasp onto the strands
of his light and mosaic those pieces together. His presence

was a neon threat we couldn't escape. His screams
        splattered over the clamoring rings of his continuous
calls after an appointment. It was so loud I could cut

my own ear off. On lackluster days, you took me on long
        drives with windows rolled down so we could color
the sky with our singing. It took you sixteen years to realize

your most precious work of art: we chose to smear over
        the pieces of him and papier macheed a fresh start.

Lady of Leisure

The hallway is long and covered in wood
that sometimes splinters and snags

at the too long, tattered-up hem of my jeans.
My bedroom is on the left but nothing

in there is mine. It was originally
a guest room. With a guest bed and guest

sheets and guest hangers for guest clothes,
and an ancient doily on the acetone

stained bedside table. Though I admit,
the acetone is mine. The doily covers

it just enough that when she pokes
her head in while I'm at school she doesn't

see. I'm not sure what she's looking
for, except proof I don't belong. The swish

of her peonied bathrobe echoes
down the hallway, avoiding the splinters.

She carries a clipboard to list each grievance.
Clothes on the floor. Bath towels hung

crooked. An unmade bed. I hear her yelling
each one at my mom when she thinks

I'm not home. She says I'm a *lady of leisure*
because don't I have better things to do

than sleep in until noon? My parents
are divorced and we gave away

the dogs that still stampede
through my dreams so we could live

here. I lost the friends I was too shy to make,
and yeah, sometimes the ache in my chest

throbs so heavy it anchors me in bed.
Grandmas are supposed to love

their grandchildren, and she does—but
I've learned from a distance is best.

Feral

Abbey, Pixel, and Murphy ate like queens.
Green beans, carrots, and roast beef
in raised bowls off the marble surface—

wouldn't want them to crane their necks.
Grandma told my sister if she wanted
to eat her steak with ketchup she might

as well eat it off the floor. Mom was
too new to being free of the punch
of my dad's voice-box to tell her to fuck

off. She was just grateful for scraps,
gift-wrapped in a glittering
doggy bag. All she knew was this roof

was a roof we wouldn't
otherwise have, and she was good
at *roll over.* We lived at ground

level, under their stomping
feet. Grandpa would clomp down
the steps, cradling and cooing

the heaviest dog in his brick wall
arms. He'd clang against the back
door to let them out and I'm sure

he did it on purpose. Waking
us with a warning—clamoring
out the *audacity* of teenagers trying

to sleep in, in *his* house. After ten years
they gifted us every single photograph
of *ourselves,* taken down from the worn

walls of their house. But the feral
faces of their three precious dogs
remain in pretty frames on every wall.

Advice From My Grandmother, From Her Perspective

It's just as easy to fall in love with a rich man as it is to fall in love with a poor man. You decided to fall in love with multiple people at the same time–none of whom are rich, nor men. The thing about homosexuals that I don't understand is their constant need to hold each other's hands, always grasping. I'm not prejudiced, there is no *phobia* in my vocabulary–I've never quaked at the sight of you (though the lilac laced through your locks is too loud). I don't like it when straight people lattice themselves together either. You gays are especially prone to shove it in my unsuspecting face. Seeing your wife in a dress was a surprise–to see her *pretty*. I'm not sorry I left your wedding early. It was too much kissing for my taste. I invited you over for dinner, but you don't come by anymore. I tell you we have the same genes, and maybe that sounds like a threat, what I mean is you are what I wish I could see in myself. I hope someday you'll miss me.

The Day I Found God in a Purple Rug

I was told that under no circumstance
was I to dye my hair
in my grandmother's home.

We lived with her, but it was never
my home—we were just permanent guests,
unwelcome ants on a picnic

blanket. There's always at least one hiding
out, searching for a scrap of something left
behind. But I am not one for rules,

and I didn't have anywhere else to go.
So, in the dead
of the 1 PM summer

afternoon
I remove everything
from the bathroom counters.

I bring in my book so I have something
to do while I wait for my hair to transition
from its dull yellow to a bright purple beacon.

I know it would be best not to move, to lessen
my chances of painting anything into a purple
permanence, proof

I was there. I grab my bright-
ass eggplant colored dye and with a practiced
hand I goop it onto my hair in grape

stained gobs. I rinse and grab the black
towel to mask any purple leakage.
After I dry my hair, I finally notice

it. The blinding white bath rug marooned
in the middle of the bathroom floor—
literally maroon now.

My lungs flutter and forget how to inflate.
I frantically flail through Google, searching
for the perfect solution to un-dye.

I empty every cupboard seeking stain remover,
vinegar, detergent, baking soda, and hope
flavored fairy dust. I run that thing

through the wash three separate times,
and even though I left my god
at my old house, I find

Him again in this moment, lurking
in that stupid stain.
He must have heard me because I un-

purpled the shit out of that rug.
I know, for her, love exists in my absence,
and one day she'll wish for a trace of me left behind.

Holy Me

It's been twelve years since I believed
I couldn't kiss
girls without being struck

down by Moroni's gold trumpet.
You told me waiting until I was eight
to get baptized meant it was my own choice

as if eight-year-olds can make a decision
about eternity. At the same age that I was
confused when you asked me to change

out of my tank top and cover
my shoulders, because my body belongs
to men, and I needed to save

them from my tempting flesh. I cloaked
myself in modesty and learned to cover
up my shame. My goodnight prayers

were passages of the Book of Mormon,
studied through the dim light
of my lava lamp, confirming

to myself and God I was worthy
of salvation. When my parents divorced,
you laid out your unwelcome mat.

Said you wanted me, but decided
you didn't want the stain
of my parents' failed marriage splashed

across the pews like wine spilled
on an altar cloth–so it was just easier
not to meet my eyes anymore.

Thank you for your unwelcome mat.
For giving me the opportunity to doubt
my faith and turn toward the benevolence
of my own angelic light. To question

the lines on those brass plates,
and the doctrine made up by you
old white men judging from atop your gilded
steeple. I've since seen through the veil

of your omnipresent bullshit, and came
out shouting my truth louder
than the testimonies poured out at the pulpit.
I wrote out my own family proclamation–

anointed myself with a family full of
fierce feminist, polyamorous queers.
Now at twenty-eight I still hesitate
at the coffee shop to decide which flavor

to add to my morning latte. I give
myself the grace to forgo any eternal
decisions. I've never felt closer to God
than now when I am wholly me.

Wholly me with my bodily temple
plastered in stained glass tattoos.
Wholly me and my eternally unfiltered
mouth, seasoning my sentences

with swears, never hesitating
to speak up and never seeking redemption
for my blasphemic proclamations.
Wholly me and my sacramental

wine Wednesdays, with my radiant
purple tarot cloth spread out over my altar,
singing psalms to the moon.
Wholly me and my sacred tenderness,

wrapping myself in the embrace
of my loves, their blushes loud enough to
drown out Moroni's gold trumpet.
Holy me.

Notes on Previous Publications

Thank you to the publications in which some of the poems in this chapbook first appeared:

Biting Back - *Anti-Heroin Chic*
Lady of Leisure - *Aurum Journal*
The Day I Found God in a Purple Rug - *Rat's Ass Review*

So Mad He Can't See Straight & Forgiveness Has Eight Wobbly Legs were first published in *Querencia's Summer 2022 Anthology*

Holy Me is forthcoming with *Resurrection Magazine*

www.ingramcontent.com/pod-product-compliance
Lightning Source LLC
Chambersburg PA
CBHW070453130626
46553CB00006B/2386